Photo credits:

Francois Gohier — Pages 6-14,19,21,22,24,26-29
Bill Curtsinger — Pages 6,8,10,15,21,26
Mauricio Handler/Wildlife Collection — Page 6
Jock Swenson/Wildlife Collection — Page 13
James B. Walshe/International Stock Photos — Page 6
Eric Martin — Page 7
Wyb Hoek/Marine Mammal Images — Page 22
Paul Ratcliffe/Marine Mammal Images — Page 9
Tom Arnborn/Marine Mammal Images — Page 9
Alejandro Robles/Marine Mammal Images — Page 28
Hal Whitehead/Marine Mammal Images — Pages 15,24
Eric Martin/Marine Mammal Images — Page 27
Janet Foster/Master File — Page 9
C. Allan Morgan — Page 12,15
Chip Matheson — Pages 13,15
Marty Snyderman — Pages 14,24,28
Chuck Davis — Pages 19,23
Kevin Schafer — Page 23
Animals Animals/Zig Leszczynski — Page 25
F. Stuart Westmorland — Front cover; Page 26

Illustration:

Robin Lee Makowski - End pages; Pages 16-17

Copyright © 1994
Kidsbooks, Inc.
3535 West Peterson Ave.
Chicago, Ill.60659

EYES ON NATURE™

WHALES & DOLPHINS

Written by
Anton Ericson

kidsbooks
Incorporated

LIVING LARGE

Spotted dolphins

It's amazing, but true. Some whales are even larger than the biggest dinosaurs were. Whales have lived on Earth for about 50 million years. As their food supply increased, whales ate more and became bigger over time. The blue whale is the largest animal that has ever lived. It can grow to 100 feet long and weigh about 300,000 pounds. That's as heavy as 25 elephants!

This baby humpback whale, swimming with its mother, might grow as long as 60 feet as an adult and weigh as much as 40 tons. ▶

FAST AND FUN ▲
When you think of dolphins, you probably think of fun. You're right! These speedsters are very playful. Ranging from about six feet to 13 feet long, dolphins like to leap clear out of the water and ride the waves made by boats.

Gray whale showing baleen in upper jaw.

6

TOOTH OR COMB
Cetaceans are grouped according to how they eat. Some have teeth that snag sea creatures. Others, like the big gray whale (left), have comblike structures called baleen. With baleen, whales can filter the sea for food and eat thousands of pounds every day. No wonder they grow to such enormous sizes!

Dolphin with teeth

SOUNDS FISHY

Although they live in water, whales and dolphins are not fish. They are mammals. Like humans, they are warm-blooded. A thick layer of fat, called blubber, helps them keep warm and survive in cold water. Also, cetaceans have lungs rather than gills. They breathe through a blowhole at the top of their head. And, they don't hatch eggs, but give birth to their babies and then nurse them on milk.

◀ This fin whale blows out water from its blowhole.

WATER PIGLETS

The porpoise probably gets its name, which means pig-fish in Latin, from being so short and chubby. Ranging from 3 to 6 feet long, most porpoises aren't as playful or as fast as dolphins. However, Dall's porpoise is known for zipping through the water and kicking up white spray.

Dall's porpoise

TOTALLY TOOTHED

The majority of whales, including all dolphins and porpoises, have teeth. But they don't chew. They swallow their food whole. In fact, most toothed whales only use their teeth to catch and hold their prey.

▲ Dusky dolphins enjoying a meal of anchovies.

◀ Common dolphins are very energetic swimmers, which helps them catch the 10 to 20 pounds of food they eat each day.

THE UNICORN LOO

It may seem incredible, but t long spear on the head of n whals is actually a tooth. Narwh have two teeth, but in the mal the one on the left side gro through the upper lip and reach up to 10 feet long. Scienti believe that it's used to attra females. Whatever its purpo this fantastic tusk gives the narw the look of a swimming unico

DEEP DIVES ▶

Beluga whales feed by diving deep into the ocean, sometimes over 1,000 feet down. There they munch on fish, squid, crabs, shrimp, clams, and worms.

ZAP AND TRAP ▼

From its large head, the sperm whale produces sound waves that stun the giant 4,000-pound squid living in the ocean depths. The whale then swallows its favorite food whole.

FANG FIGHTS

The male sperm whale uses his teeth to fight other males during mating season. The 24 to 30 cone-shaped teeth on each side of the lower jaw grow up to seven inches long and weigh as much as two pounds each.

This sperm whale tooth was scrimshawed, or engraved, in 1877 by whalers.

WHALE HUNGRY ▼

Killer whales definitely use their 50 cone-shaped teeth to chew. Also known as *orcas,* a name that comes from Orcus, the Roman god of the underworld, these killers can cut a seal in half. Traveling in packs, they will attack not only fish, but also big baleen whales, dolphins, porpoises, manatees, turtles, and penguins.

FILTER FEEDERS

It may seem odd, but there are 10 kinds of whales that don't have any teeth at all. Hanging from their upper jaws are rows of bristled strands called baleen. Made of a material similar to the human fingernail, the baleen acts as a food filter.

Baleen

▲ A humpback whale feeding (note baleen).

SQUEEZE PLAY

Baleen whales eat by taking in a mouthful of water and then "spitting" it out. Anything too large to squeeze through the baleen, such as krill, anchovies, sardines, and herring, is left behind to be swallowed.

KRILL-A-PLENTY

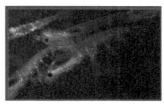

The favorite food of most baleen whales is krill—orange sea creatures that look like shrimp and grow up to two inches long. Scientists estimate there may be six and a half billion tons in the Antarctic Ocean alone! A blue whale eats more than nine tons of krill every day.

SUPER SCOOPERS

Gray whales do not gulp their food. Living close to the shore in the Pacific Ocean, they swim to the bottom of the sea and lie on their side. There they scoop up a mouthful of mud and then force it back out through their baleen. What's left behind is a dinner of crabs and clams.

GULPING GOODIES

Fin whales, as well as blue, Bryde's, humpback, sei, and minke whales, are specially equipped to take huge gulps of krill and fish at one time. On their throats, there are grooves, or pleats, that stretch to allow the throat to expand.

◀ Fin whales feeding on a school of herring.

▼ A humpback's bubble net.

▲
Humpback whales also feed by *lunging* into a school of fish that they've herded into a ball.

BUBBLE TROUBLE

Because humpback whales prefer fish to krill, they sometimes eat in a special way, called bubble-net feeding. The humpback blows air from its blowhole as it swims in a spiral below a school of fish. The bubbles rise in a "net," surrounding the frightened fish. The whale then swims inside the net of bubbles, catching the trapped fish.

THE TALE OF TAILS

Whales and dolphins propel themselves through the water with their tails, which have two strong wings, or *flukes*. Instead of wagging their flukes from side to side like fish, they move them up and down in powerful strokes.

A sperm whale's huge, triangular ▶ flukes are 16 feet across.

The blue whale's 23-foot-long ▶ flukes are relatively small for such an enormous animal.

Humpbacks raise their flukes when diving.
▼

Fin

Tail

Flipper

The humpback whale's flippers are sometimes one-third the length of its entire body.

FABULOUS FLIPPERS

Whales have flippers on each side at the front of their body. In prehistoric days, before whales moved into the water, these flippers were used for walking on land. Whale flippers are now used for steering, braking, and sometimes to knock away an attacker, but not for swimming.

A killer whale's dorsal fin ▲ can grow up to six feet.

The beluga is one of the few ▶ whales without a dorsal fin.

FINTASTIC

Most whales have a stiff fin on their back that helps them stay on course while swimming. Depending on the whale, this dorsal fin can be small or large.

The huge fin whale, which can grow ▶ up to 80 feet, has a tiny dorsal fin.

AIR HEAD

Baleen whales, like the gray whale, have two blowholes.

Looking at a whale, you wouldn't think it had a nose. But it does. Whales have nostrils, called blowholes. Over millions of years of evolution, whales' nostrils moved to the top of their head, allowing them to breathe by surfacing, rather than by sticking their whole head out of the water.

▲Toothed whales, like this dolphin, have only one blowhole.

The blue whale ▶ shoots a single, thin jet 40 to 50 feet high.

◀ The gray whale blows out a bushy plume 10 to 13 feet high.

BLOW UP

When a whale comes to the surface and exhales, water in the blowhole and moisture in the whale's breath bursts into the air in a marvelous spout. Because whales have different shaped blowholes, they have different shaped spouts.

▲ A right whale sends out two, 16-foot spouts in a V-shape.

ROCK HEAD ▶

Whales do not have completely smooth skin. They are covered with barnacles, worms, lice, and colorful algae. Barnacles grow thickly on gray whales, giving them the appearance of having a rocky surface.

On the right whale, there is a distinctive patch of barnacles, worms, and lice called a "bonnet" or "rock garden." The head accounts for 40% of the whale's entire length.

Blue whale

Sperm whale

BIG HEAD

Some whales have very large heads compared to the rest of their body. Their necks are stiff to keep their large heads steady while they're swimming. For this reason, most whales cannot turn their head from side to side.

A blue whale is one-fourth head and three-fourths body.

The head of a sperm whale is easy to recognize. It is 20-feet long, 10-feet high, and 7-feet wide. Its tooth-filled jaw is 16 feet long.

Right whale

WHALE WATCH

Shown here in relation to one another by size, whales and dolphins vary greatly in shape and color.

Orca

Right Whale

Rough-Toothed Dolphin

Fin Whale

Common Dolphins

Risso's Dolphin

Humpback Whale

Hector's Dolphin

False Killer Whale

Harbor Porpoise

Bottlenose Dolphin

Blue Whale

Spotted Dolphins

Northern Bottlenose Whale

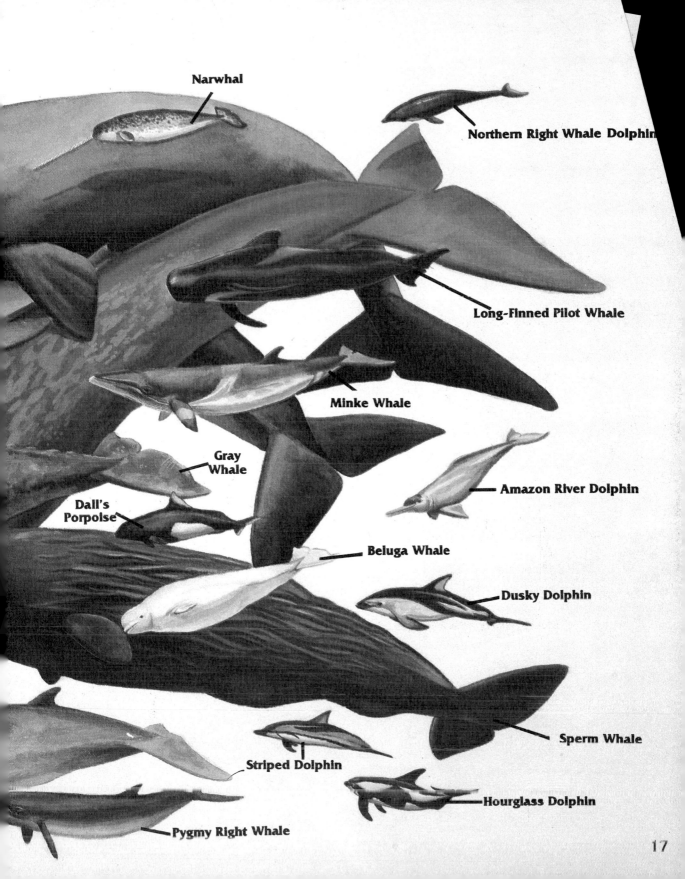

Narwhal

Northern Right Whale Dolphin

Long-Finned Pilot Whale

Minke Whale

Gray Whale

Amazon River Dolphin

Dall's Porpoise

Beluga Whale

Dusky Dolphin

Striped Dolphin

Sperm Whale

Hourglass Dolphin

Pygmy Right Whale

17

WHAT A BABY!

A baby whale, called a calf, is extremely close to its mother. From the moment of its underwater birth, a calf is totally dependent on her. The two will spend many months together, sometimes years, before the young calf can take care of itself.

The birth of an orca. ▲

A gray whale mother and her calf surface together for air. ▲

SINK OR SWIM

The first thing a newborn whale must do is go to the surface for air, even though it cannot yet swim. Its mother and sometimes another female whale will help it to the surface. Within about a half hour, the baby will be able to swim on its own.

COPY CAT CALF

Calves learn by imitating. They turn, dive, and surface right along with their mother. But whale mothers aren't just teachers. They're also playmates. Gray whale mothers play a special game with their babies. They swim underneath them and blow bubbles out their blowhole. This sends little whales into a spin.

This family of spotted dolphins keeps ▲ their baby under protective cover.

This mother whale and her calf ▼ come up above water for a look around.

BABY LOVE

Because calves are very playful, they sometimes get into trouble. Often aunts will help take care of them, but mothers still watch their babies closely. When a calf disobeys, its mother butts it with her head. She also protects her baby by using her flippers to hold it close to her body.

▲ This baby beluga sticks close to its mother.

FREE RIDE

Calves follow closely at their mother's side. Some keep up by riding their mother's waves and underwater currents. The flow of water over the mother's body helps pull the calf along. For a really easy ride, babies will hang on to their mother's fin.

BABY BLUES

Whale babies grow quickly on their mother's rich milk. Blue whale babies grow the fastest of all. At birth, they can be as long as 23 feet and weigh as much as two tons. They will drink about 44 gallons of milk a day and gain seven pounds an hour. Usually, blue whales grow until they're about 30 years old, and they live to be 60 to 80 years old.

19

WATER SPORTS

Whales, as big as they are, swim with unusual grace. But swimming is not all they can do. Whales perform aquabatics. They breach, lobtail, sail, surf, and spyhop. Some scientists think that the noise made from lobtailing and breaching may be another way whales communicate. But, maybe it's just whale play.

LOBTAILING ▲

Without warning, a lobtailing whale suddenly points itself straight down into the water. It raises its huge flukes into the air, wags them playfully back and forth a few times, and then slaps them against the water with a sound as loud as a cannon shot. Whales also raise their flukes into the air like sails and glide just beneath the surface on wind power.

Humpback whale

SPYHOPPING

A spyhopping whale sticks its head straight out of the water like a giant periscope and holds it there for 30 seconds or more. It looks around, sometimes turning a full circle, and then disappears. Then it sometimes comes back to do it all over again.

RACING AND CHASING

Dolphins like to swim fast. When a speeding boat passes by, they'll race out in front and ride its bow waves. When racing each other, they'll first leap into the air and then take off after hitting the water. Dolphins also play tag and dance on their tails across the water's surface.

▲ These bottlenose dolphins fly high above the sea.

◀ A spotted dolphin leaps clear of the water and skirts the surface.

▼ SURFING

Right whales swim upstream into strong tidal currents. When they stop swimming, the current sweeps them back to where they started—to do it all over again. Imagine a body-surfer 60-feet long!

BREACHING

To breach, a whale first dives underwater, then throws itself straight up into the air, as high as it can. Some even leap clear of the water. But whales cannot fly, so they fall back into the sea with a loud splash that can be heard for miles.

ALL IN THE FAMILY

Most whales are fairly social and like to live in groups. These herds, or *pods*, vary in number and consist of family members and friends. Beluga whales usually live in Arctic waters in large groups that number up to 1,000. However, every few years one or two will follow cold currents as far south as New York City.

◄ A pod of beluga whales.

A pod ► of orcas.

ROUND-TRIP TRAVELERS

◄ Many whales migrate constantly, traveling from one region to another to find food, breed, and have their young. Each spring, gray whales leave their winter breeding grounds off the coast of Baja California. They head to the Arctic Ocean, where they feed on krill. In September, they start south again, swimming 24 hours a day to reach their favorite lagoon in time to have their young. The round-trip journey is over 12,000 miles.

BUDDY BAILOUT ▶
Dolphins swim in large herds hat sometimes number more than ,000. They also associate with ther whales, such as the right, umpback, and gray whales. Within these groups, dolphins ook out after one another. When anger approaches, they send sigals. If one member is injured or in listress, they will push it to the urface so it can breathe.

HOME, HOME ON THE SEA
Whales and dolphins live in all the world's oceans and some of its rivers, as well. Some live far out to sea while others hug the shore.

Found in all the world's oceans, from the tropics to the Arctic, orcas usually live in pods numbering 3 to 30, but sometimes they travel in larger herds that number 100.

IERD HUNGER
iroup living is safer when enenies like sharks and killer whales re nearby. It also makes it easier or some whales to find and catch ood. Species like these humpback vhales sometimes gather in large ;roups and drive fish into a conentrated area. This is called cooprative feeding.

INVISIBLE MAPS
Whales and dolphins navigate by following the hills and valleys on the ocean floor, by tracking the sun, by sensing ocean currents, and by tasting the water from rivers and bays along their journey. They also detect changes in the earth's magnetic field, a sense that acts like an internal compass. This "compass" helps them through even dark, murky water.

SEA SIGHTS AND SOUNDS

Gray whale

Right whales have eyes ▶ the size of grapefruits.

CRY BABIES

Whales have no eyelids. They rely on thick, oily tears to protect their eyes from the effects of seawater and air. Captured dolphins give the impression they are crying. But they aren't. Their tears are flowing to protect their sensitive eyes from drying out.

PINHOLE WONDERS Although they have no ears on the outside of their heads, whales and dolphins have excellent hearing. Tiny pinholes, as narrow as a pencil, are located just behind their eyes. Through these holes, they can pick up sounds from many miles away.

Much of the sea is dark all of the time. To get around safely, find food, and to locate one another, whales and dolphins have developed keen senses. Scientists disagree about how well whales can see. Some think they have poor above-water vision and good underwater vision. Others think they see quite well above and below water.

WHALE TALK

The sea is not as silent as it seems. Whales talk to one another by making whistles, clicks, squeaks, squawks, rattles, and groans. People can hear these sounds, too. Male humpback whales sing "songs," which have been taped. People listen to these recordings as they would any other kind of music.

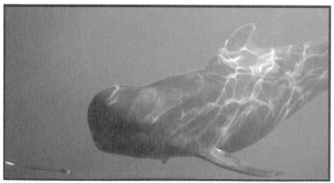

◀ This pilot whale, right behind the mike, tells all.

ECHO VISION

Like bats, toothed whales can make sounds to "see" what lays ahead. This sense is called *echolocation*. The whale's sound waves hit an object, such as a school of fish, and the echo bounces back. Echolocation sounds, called *spray,* are so strong that they can stun things, such as fish or other whales. From early on, whales and dolphins learn that they must never "point" their melons toward other whales.

▼ To avoid spraying each other these dolphins swim side by side.

▼ These belugas hang out without pointing their melons at each other.

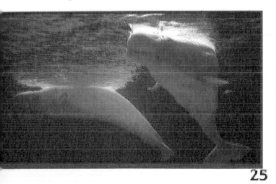

A REAL WATER MELON

A whale's sounds probably originate in its nasal passages. The large forehead, or melon, found on some whales, like on this bottlenose dolphin, is thought to focus the sounds.

ORCA

LIFETIME COMPANIONS

Orca pods are very much lik
close families. An orca spends i
whole life in the same group an
continues to stay attached to i
mother. Each pod may also hav
its own specific way of living
choosing to eat certain things an
communicating in ways slightl
different from other pods.

FIN TOWERS

How can you tell male
and female orcas apart?
Male killer whales have really tall—up to six feet—
dorsal fins. Females and
young orcas have smaller,
curved fins that resemble
those of dolphins.

KILLER CAPERS

Like dolphins, orcas love to
play. Although they can weigh
as much as 18,000 pounds and
grow to 32 feet, they are very
athletic. Killer whales can swim
30 miles per hour and can leap
and turn quickly. These talents
are what makes them so dan-
gerous. They fear nothing and
can chase down almost any sea
creature.

▲ TRUE, FALSE KILLERS

Unlike orcas, false killer whales are all
black and slender. Sometimes people con-
fuse them with female orcas because their
fins are short and hooked.

A spyhopping ▶
killer whale.

This breaching orca shows off its
distinctive white patches.

LIFE'S TOO SHORT

Many people believe that orcas should not be held in captivity. In acquariums, orcas tend to live for about 13 years. Compared to those in the wild, who live for 40 to 60 years, their lifetime in captivity is much too short.

This mother and calf ▶ perform a double breach.

IN THE TANK

Orcas, like dolphins, are easily trained. They have large brains and are very intelligent. They are affectionate and gentle, too, and usually cooperate with trainers. Because of their wondrous performances at marine parks, orcas have helped to strengthen the whale protection movement.

KILLING TIME

Some people wonder if the bond formed between trainers and orcas adequately replaces the whales' social life in the wild. They do enjoy having their rubbery skin petted by human hands. But sometimes orcas become so bored that they think up tricks of their own just to kill time.

This killer whale is hanging out with a trainer friend.

27

Right whale

Many dolphins and porpoises ge trapped in fishing nets. Unable t surface and breathe air, the wate mammals drown. *Drift nets,* som big enough to encircle the city o New York, are set for fish but catc everything. Because the fisherme want only the fish, they simply thro the bodies of the dead dolphins an porpoises back overboard.

WHALES AND PEOPLE

Because of their size and speed, whales have few natural enemies besides humans. In the 19th century, people hunted whales to near extinction for oil, baleen, and meat. Baleen was used like plastic is today, in products like brushes and corsets. A few nations still practice whaling, but most have now stopped.

Right whales were first hunted in 12th-century Spain. They are now in danger of extinction.

▼ The vaquita porpoise, like th one, is a common victim of the fisherman's ne There are only a fev hundred still living

TOXIC WATERS

Pollution is the greatest threat whales face today. Oil spills, toxic wastes, and sewage dumping affect the foods that whales eat and become toxins in their systems. Some scientists believe that pollution harms the whale's navigating system, causing some to swim into shallow waters and wash ashore.

These beached pilot ▲ whales are being kept wet by a friendly human.

◄ A researcher rescues a harbor porpoise from a herring net.

An injured humpback whale.

n 1988, these volunteers chopped a hole in
he Alaskan ice to free two gray whales that
vere trapped.

NYLON NICKS

Even nylon fishing lines that float
on the sea can severly injure dolphins and whales. The animal gets
entangled, and the line cuts through
its flesh, sometimes cutting off the
dorsal fin.

FRIENDLY FOLKS

Many people and organi-
zations are now working to
secure a safer future for
dolphins and whales.

MAMMAL GET-TOGETHER

Whale-watching groups
go out to sea in hope of
meeting whales. Getting
close to these magnificent
mammals is an exciting
experience.